JOANNE HAMMIL

Rounds & Partner Songs

Volume

SONGBOOK

Music engraved by **Janet Hood**

◆

Design by **Alison Tolman-Rogers**

◆

Cover Art: Pelagia Colorata, by **L Carlene Raper**
Bedquilt of hand-dyed cotton fabrics (www.colorquilts.com)

Contents

Forward

Rounds and partner songs are based on the harmonies and joys of counterpoint or polyphony: that is, music made up of independent lines flowing alongside each other and continually merging in different ways – creating ever new turns, interesting perspectives and beautiful joinings.

I have been intrigued by counterpoint all my life in the smallest and broadest senses. I delight in rounds and other polyphonic musical styles, take joy in individuals singing and playing music together, and am fascinated by the ways different peoples live and work together in a family, a community, a country, a world.

Definitions:

In these collections of my original Rounds & Partner Songs, I've included several contrapuntal song forms, some of which overlap in their definitions. There is a lot of incomplete and conflicting information about these song forms, even in the many text books, writings and other sources that I've explored in my research. Part of this is because definitions have changed somewhat over the centuries, and part of it is due to the confusion of overlapping definitions. It is also true that many contrapuntal musical forms were created and experimented with in delightful ways throughout history, and it is only when scholars began to categorize and define them that the confines of the definitions did not always fit correctly. For those musicians or listeners like myself to whom even some of the basic differences in these forms have often seemed confusing, I offer my conclusions in the following definitions:

NOTE: Succinct, short definitions of these forms are included in the booklet of the companion CD to this Songbook. They are perhaps easier to grasp for those not interested in a lot of detail.

CANON: The word "canon" comes from the Greek *kanon*, meaning "rule" or "order". In music, a canon refers to a polyphonic piece which has a specific rule by which a composer constructs the successive voices to derive from the first. There are many kinds of canons: some with voices entering at different pitches (canon at the fifth or fourth, etc.), and some that are extremely complex, involving backward or upside down imitation, or imitation with notes of greater or shorter durations.

There are even those called riddle canons in which the rule of imitation is not written out and must be deciphered by the singers/players. Many canons are incorporated within instrumental pieces and others stand as independent vocal or instrumental creations.

ROUND: Rounds are a subset of canons. A "round" is generally a lighter canon for singing whose 'rule' is simply that the successive voices follow the first in exact imitation on the same notes at a set time interval, continuing over and over until an arbitrary end point. Each voice returns to the beginning after singing the song through, and so the piece turns *around* in a circle. In musical canon jargon, a round is an infinite canon (no set ending) at the unison (beginning on the same pitch).

NOTE about "round" vs "canon": The terms "round" and "canon" are often used interchangeably, though there are *many* canons that are not rounds. Songs with exact imitation of the first voice are often referred to as canons rather than rounds when one or both of the following two conditions are met:
1) successive parts enter *quickly* in imitation, perhaps after only a few beats or a measure or two (and therefore do not necessarily divide the entire song into long sections of phrases that all harmonize with each other), and
2) the piece has a finite ending, with notes added to some parts to create this set ending.

In this collection, I am choosing to refer to all songs with exact imitation of parts as rounds.

CATCH: Often used synonymously with "round" when the lyrics are lighthearted, the "catch" grew out of the related forms *chace* (French) *caccia* (Italian) and *caça* (Spanish) and originally simply referred to one or more voices chasing the others and/or the way each singer catches the tune and words from the previous voice. Over time, however, the catch developed a distinct propensity for hidden meanings or other non-musical points (punning, programmatic content, etc.). Catches became more cleverly constructed, especially through the 17th century, to involve intricate interplay of the different voice parts so that new word combinations were audible only as all the parts were being sung. Historically, they also became more crude and bawdy so that the hidden words that popped out as the catch was sung were often comic or off-color.

PARTNER SONG: The term "partner song", sometimes called "quodlibet", has 2 basic meanings:
1) Two or more totally independent songs that by chance happen to have the same harmonic structure and therefore can be sung together at the same time.
2) A song written intentionally with different independent lines that all harmonize with each other to form an interlocking 'partnership'.

AFRICAN-STYLE CYCLICAL SONG: This form is modeled on a kind of cyclical song found in many African cultures in which each part is independent – with its own unique melody, lyrics, rhythmic structure and even *entry* point within the cycles – yet all parts converge on the same few syllables at one point in each repeat. The continuous short cycles of separation into very different lines and then convergence together are what drives this vibrant form and makes it a delight to sing with a group. It is a very specific and unique kind of partner song.

About singing rounds – important arrangement considerations:

When singing rounds, there are many factors to consider that affect the sound considerably. In the companion recording to this songbook, the decisions about these factors were carefully made for each round, but many other choices would also have sounded lovely, so I encourage lots of experimentation with the following variables:

1) Rounds will sound quite different depending on the **octave range** and therefore the order of female/male voices, as that changes the interval structures throughout the song.

2) They will sound very different depending on the **number of parts** used. A round can begin with two parts, for example, and then add successive parts in later cycles, or all parts can enter as soon as possible and create the fullest sound possible from the start. Some rounds, especially those with many short parts, actually might sound *preferable* when sung with fewer parts because that allows the sounds to follow in a changing wave throughout the song, and avoids having every short phrase sound identical and somewhat "thick".

3) The **order of the entering voices** affects the sound dramatically. Singing every *other* part first – and then adding the intervening parts in later cycles – creates an interesting kind of "space" and harmonic relationship that is appealing in some rounds. This is quite different from the immediate fullness one hears when all the parts enter right away in their numeric order. I like to start some 4-part rounds in the part order 1-3-2-4. By the second cycle, all the parts will be in anyway, but the beginning spaciousness can be intriguing.

4) There is always an interesting decision to be made about **how to end a round**: parts can drop out as they complete their last cycle, or they can keep going until a designated moment when all parts end together chordally. If they drop out, they can either stay out or continue in a variety of ways: they can keep repeating their last phrase so all parts end together in unison, they can hum or "ooh" until all parts finish, they can simply rejoin the last line of the last part for a full unison ending, or they can re-enter with a harmonized coda, or some other set ending.

5) **Whether to accompany** a round with instrumentation or sing it acapella is an interesting decision to make. With accompaniment, one risks obscuring the rich counterpoint of the voices, but the resulting 'grounding' and enhancement that accompaniment can provide is often worth that risk.

Tips about learning and singing rounds:

1) Sing in a circle when possible, with all parts facing each other. This not only provides the best acoustics for hearing all the parts, but helps singers hear the flow of the cycling melodies and harmonies.

2) Try practicing without words, on a common vowel sound like "du" or "na" when striving to create a good harmonic blend; the harmonies might lock in more tightly than when every part is singing different words with different consonant and vowel sounds.

3) Hearing a round played instrumentally will also reveal the harmonies better for the same reason: it eliminates the distortion of the pure tones of the chords from the singers' different consonants and vowels occurring in their different parts at the same time. Once the harmonies are heard clearly, it is sometimes easier to line up vocal sounds more exactly.

4) Try standing in many small groups (quartets for 4-part rounds, trios for 3, etc.) with all the "Part 1" people beginning first and all the "Part 2" people next, etc. It can be very exciting to hear single voices creating a round within a small group, while still being supported by the others in the room who are singing the same parts.

5) Adding movement while singing some rounds can be very exciting:
   a) Have everyone start walking randomly around the room after all the parts are going, singing to others they greet or pass.
   b) Create choreography for the different lines of a piece and watch the cycling flow of similar movements add a visual element to the counterpoint.

6) Try singing one cycle (the 3rd time through the round, for example) on "ooh" (no words) and then bring the words back in on the next cycle. This can add variety to any song, but in *rounds* singing, the staggered changes to "ooh" and back to words are particularly effective. It can also be a lovely way to end a round, rolling the words into "oohs" for each part's final cycle.

7) Here are variations of #6 above, which add a different sound to one cycle in the middle of a round:
   a) Use kazoos for one cycle (particularly effective on upbeat jazzy rounds).
   b) Use rhythm instruments or clapping for one cycle, following the rhythm with no melody.
   c) Use silent hand motions or sign language for one cycle, keeping the rhythm internally, so that all sound drops out and the piece cycles through just visually in the middle of the round.

8) Sing very softly for practice sometimes. This helps remind everyone to avoid out-singing other parts in order to hear their own, and encourages listening more intently to the interrelationship of all the parts.

9) To hear the beauty of the whole round with balanced parts, take turns standing in the center of the rounds singers simply to listen. In rehearsals with large groups, I often just leave an empty chair in the middle and people can get up and sit there when so moved.

10) Although equal volume in all parts is generally a good goal for balancing parts, there are phrases in some songs that sound great when they are brought out strongly. Try swelling on certain lines so you hear that line emerging and cascading through the piece as each group sings it.

11) Having a leader in front of each part is very helpful when singing with a new group or a large group of people. When singing rounds with young children, use individual children as leaders of each part. They don't need to be individuals who know the round best or even sing it in tune well! Young children simply do better with a visual focus to maintain their independent parts. In fact, the members of each part will keep their "leader" on track and on pitch as much as the other way around, but the leaders will enable the children to be clear about sticking to their part within the whole.

12) Rounds provide a perfect "take off" for vocal improvisation. Since they are made up of single melodic lines that work together harmonically, the singers are already "soloing" in a way while listening and blending with others. After singing a round through several cycles, try improvising on a phrase or a word or a whole sentence from the round while everyone keeps singing. Each singer randomly can begin to improvise, holding to the harmonic structure that was the "bed" of the round. Flights of phrases that loop around and join others in fanciful improvised counterpoint are easy to experiment with while singing rounds. Try a simple ostinato, a higher descant, or even a drone part. If everyone is "tuned in" and really listening to each other, the piece will, at some point, come to a natural and satisfying group close.

Notes about the music notation in this book:

1) Numbers and Parts
Within the rounds, Arabic numbers indicate the points at which each part starts singing in relation to Part 1 *from the beginning* of the round.

Within the partner songs, Roman numerals indicate the beginning of *each separate part*.

2) Staff Connection
In notating rounds, the staves don't *need* to be connected in order to sing the piece, as each part sings through from the first note to the last, but I chose to connect the staves with a single left system line for two reasons:

a) I notated the rounds so that the measures line up vertically to reveal the harmonic structure, and so the connecting system line helps one visualize how all the parts are connected by chord structure. This chordal line up also allowed me to add chord markings as an aid for possible accompaniments.

b) Since some of the rounds have longer lines between parts, they require two systems. A system line is then necessary to indicate that Part 1 continues on the next *system* rather than the next *staff.* Using a system line on all the rounds, therefore, whether they require two systems or not, makes the notation for rounds consistent throughout the book.

In partner songs, the systems (groups of staves) are bracketed together, indicating that, after the initial singing of each part separately, *the parts each start at the beginning of their own line and at the same time.* This is standard notation for parts in choral music.

3) Partner song structure
On all partner songs, each part should of course sing their line independently first before all parts sing simultaneously.

NOTE: Many of the partner songs included in this collection can also be sung as rounds, simply by having each voice sing through all the parts instead of repeating just one line. These songs are marked "partner song or round". The decision of whether to *notate* a particular song that has this dual possibility as a partner song or as a round was made to match the way I chose to perform the song on the companion recording.

4) Chord markings
Chord markings are given for all songs but are often useful only for *learning* the songs (with accompaniment) or simply for understanding the harmonic structure of the piece. Sometimes instrumental accompaniment can obscure the rich contrapuntal singing that is the essence of rounds and other times accompaniment can greatly enhance the piece. I include chord markings so the reader has that option, depending on the group that is singing and the desired effect.

On a few songs, alternate chord markings are suggested in parentheses on subsequent lines (after the first), to add variety to a possible accompaniment and to match what was played on the companion recording.

5) Tempo markings
Tempo markings are included simply as a suggestion and to match the performance on the companion recording to this songbook.

6) Codas and specific endings
I have notated Codas and specific endings to match the way I chose to perform these songs on the companion recording. These endings are meant only as guides and suggestions. Choosing how to end a particular round is an interesting, creative task that will depend a lot on the particular group of singers and what effect is desired.

7) Number of parts notated
Occasionally a round is marked with an ambiguous designation such as "4-11 part round". This happens in rounds with many short parts to indicate that although the piece does harmonize as an 11-part round, it might be more effective to sing in fewer parts. By having only 4 parts sing in quick succession, the sounds will flow in waves and patterns through the piece rather than remain static with each short phrase being identical. All 11 parts are notated, however, with Arabic numbers. Starting with fewer parts and then adding the full number of possible parts in later cycles can be very exciting.

8) Lyrics layout
The full lyrics to each song are included after the music. These lyrics are formatted to match the way the musical lines and vocal parts enter. For those who don't read music or want to just sing by following the words, they can easily see where each part begins and how the parts line up. For a more poetic formatting of the lyrics for each song, see the booklet with the companion CD to this songbook. There, the lyrics are laid out by poetic line, with circled numbers indicating the point at which each part starts singing from the beginning of the round.

For questions about arrangements or to clarify notated intent, contact JHO Music at www.joannehammil.com.

I'm excited to share my joy of counterpoint in this collection, as well as send my own compositions out into the blend of our combined, interweaving voices.

Joanne Hammil

Song Notes...

NOW THAT I KNOW *The harmonies in this round alternate between major and minor chords to reflect the juxtaposition of loss and fulfillment in the lyrics, while the melody lines swell and flow to convey the overall positive sentiment.*

SHOULD I? *The first two musical parts dovetail in the beginning to accentuate the back-and-forth mental questioning, so keeping a strict beat and a clipped articulation is essential here. It can be equally effective to sing this as four people interrelating about making a decision, or as four completely separate people, each lost in their own personal indecision.*

TAKE ME AWAY *The form of this song is one common to many African community songs (in which the separate parts converge on a phrase once in every short cycle), but it otherwise doesn't sound African at all. Instead, the melodic lines are smooth and flowing as they weave around each other, portraying the flow of the river and the singers' yearning to be carried away.*

RULES *This round is quite easy for even very young children to sing well if you eliminate the 2-part ending: simply have Part 1 join Part 2 on its last phrase ("to show that I'm important like you!"), then all fold their arms, nod their heads, and say "Hmmph!".*

MOVE LIKE JAZZ *I wrote this with an evocative, "smoky", romantic edge because it's about my love affair with dance. Try dancing it! One dancer or three dancers can choreograph each of the three parts as they are first sung alone, and then make the dance ideas merge as the vocal parts are merged together. It's especially effective if the singers change to "ooh", instead of the lyrics, for a middle verse in which dancers can take a more active, solo role.*

RUTABAGA *Written in the unique style of many African community songs, this is particularly fun to sing, as the focal word "rutabaga" is so peculiar and funny. The dramatic, strong statements, in a minor key, make the piece even more ironic.*

ME AND YOU *This partner song is the chorus of a song in which the verses are examples of challenging pairings: two different cultures, ages, and any other kind of dichotomy (sexes, races, etc). The chorus can be sung between the verses first as separate solo parts and later as the full partner song.*

LEFT, RIGHT *A play on the words "left" and "right" on many levels, this round should be performed while marching in place, beginning with left foot. Whenever the word "left" is sung, you'll be landing on left foot; when "right" is sung, you'll be landing on right foot. This helps keep you on track as well as enhance the playfulness.*

KATE'S FULL MOON SING *Written after the first time I participated in one of Kate Munger's lovely rounds sings.*

FOR PETE'S SAKE *Written in tribute to a true mentor of mine, with many hidden references to the subject of the catch: the whistle in the beginning, banjo accompaniment, mention of Sing Out! magazine, his philosophies, etc. The separation of the word "girl" into two false syllables is a little strange to sing but makes the whole 'catch' work!*

DON'T GIVE UP *This is a great song for group singing, as the belief in the power of the people is emphasized by the exciting form of this piece. All parts converge once in every short cycle on one phrase. If the singers actually lean in toward the other groups on that converging phrase each time it comes around, they will feel the power they are singing about!*

ROLL IT OVER *A friend made a casual comment that I loved, about the fact that all of life is Plan B. I couldn't resist creating a round based on that idea and the need to simply just roll with things at times. I wrote this music to literally 'roll over and over' as the 8 parts keep somersaulting after each other in quick canonic succession.*

TOSHI'S CLAM CHOWDER *I wrote this song in the style of many African community songs (in which all parts keep converging on one phrase) as a "thank you" to Toshi for a fabulous lunch. It seemed fitting to honor her great homemade soup by having the singers keep meshing on the words "Toshi's clam chowder", in an almost regal fashion.*

MORNING RHYTHMS *Each line of this rhythm round gets a little more urgent and "hurried" in affect. Then, as it grows into a 3-part, syncopated rhythm piece, the escalating frenzy of sound echoes the rising pace of rhythms within a morning household, right up to that last dash for the school bus.*

SOMETIMES I STUMBLE *I wrote this round for Ben Tousley, in September 1997, to celebrate that he had been free of cancer for 5 years.*

HERE I AM! *Written while driving to a friend's house in 1995, as I took time out of a busy work tour in Northern California to enjoy the greater importance of connecting with a dear friend.*

I CAN'T SING *The rhythms of the first two parts of this partner song came from a workshop by Ubaka Hill on African drumming. They are two common rhythms often played together to create a polyrhythmic base of sound. I set words to these rhythms so that singers could easily enjoy this same effect. It's exciting to have each part played on a rhythm instrument while singing. At some point drop the voices out but keep the instruments going; then the voices can rejoin the instruments for a full finish.*

HAPPY BIRTHDAY ROUND *I wrote this round in a joyous, calypso style, which resulted in a birthday song that begs to be danced to.*

YES, NO *This partner song becomes an interesting game to play with an intergenerational crowd. After singing the different parts according to people's age groups, switch parts and experience the different perspectives. It's even more powerful and fun to all walk randomly around the room, declaratively singing with gusto to each other.*

A MOTHER'S HAPPINESS *A simple melody, that begins with the poignant interval of a rising 7th to express the pain of this simple statement.*

ASSUMPTIONS *Missed cues, wrong assumptions – it's a subject I had fun working into the form of a round, as the singers each declare the same erroneous thoughts at different times.*

FUZZY WUZZY *It's fun to sing this tongue-twister round faster and faster and to tack on the 2-part coda at super speed!*

EASY AS MI SOL DO *This is a piece that sounds complex but is just made up of two simple ostinati and two counter melodies. Children have no trouble mastering the four parts.*

HOPE *The tied notes in the beginning of the second line make this simple round very satisfying to sing when the two parts are tightly synchronized.*

TOO MUCH *The music is a bit "too much", reflecting the words. It's quite difficult to line up these parts but lots of fun to sing when you do.*

ON THE MOVE *A round with changing verses presents unique performance challenges. In order to hear the words of the different verses, I like to sing the first few verses in unison and then break into the 4-part round for verses 4 and 5.*

Now That I Know

Words & Music by
Joanne Hammil

4-part round

Now that I know what wings are for I can no longer fly.

Now that I know what vi-sion brings I do not have my eyes; but

now that I know the mo-ments are the sweet-est parts of all —

I don't need wings or eyes that see to cher-ish ___ it all.

Now that I know what wings are for I can no longer fly.

Now that I know what vision brings I do not have my eyes; But

Now that I know the moments are the sweetest parts of all —

I don't need wings or eyes that see to cherish it all.

Should I?

Words & Music by
Joanne Hammil

4-part round

* Indicates where each part drops out on last cycle

Should I? Should I not? The moment of decision is upon me. I

Just don't know; I can't decide; maybe I should, on the other hand I could be

Making a terrible mistake: but if I don't act it could be

Worse! 'cause that's like making a choice without choosing, which is really dumb so

Should I?

Take Me Away

3-part African-style cyclical song

Words & Music by
Joanne Hammil

♩ = 126

Am   *Fine*   **C**   **G**   **F**   **G**   **Am**

I *Part I start here - repeat this line only*

1. Riv - er *take __ me a - way, __*   a - way   to   the   o - cean. __

Fine   **II** *Part II start here - repeat this line only*

take,   *take __ me a - way. __*   2. Car - ry   me   a - way   on your cur - rent;   oh

Fine   **III** *Part III start here - repeat this line only*

please   *take __ me a - way __*   to   the   o - cean. 3. Oh   riv - er won't __ you

1. River take me away, away to the ocean.

2. Carry me away on your current — oh take, take me away.

3. Oh river won't you please take me away to the ocean.

Rules

Words & Music by
Joanne Hammil

2-part round

How can I follow all the rules that you make, if I don't get to make some too? If
You let me make some I won't have to break some to show that I'm important like you!

ending:

To show that I'm important, show that I'm important,

Show that I'm important like you!

10

Move Like Jazz

Words & Music by
Joanne Hammil

3-part partner song or round

1. Each time I start to dance I know the world will keep on turning forever;

   It makes me take a chance — turning my heartbeats into rhythm.

2. Step by step I move, opening up my heart, my mind, all I know;

   Moving as one with all I feel — even the truth I used to know.

3. Stepping into time I turn with the power dance has;

   Stepping in my mind I smile as I move like jazz.

Rutabaga

4-part African-style cyclical song

Words & Music by
Joanne Hammil

1. Broccoli, kale, rutabaga, brussel sprouts.

2. Mama says to eat your vegetables — even — guess what? Rutabaga!

3. Who would name a food rutabaga?!

4. Believe it or not — rutabaga tastes good!

Me And You

Words & Music by
Joanne Hammil

Song whose chorus is a 2-part partner song

♩ = 125

chorus:

I **D**

Would you like a glass of wat-er? Would you like to sit down? Would you like to talk a lit-tle with

II

Tell me — what's your name? _ What do you like to

A **G** **D** **F#** **Bm** **D/A** **Em/A**

me? I know I'm dif-f'rent — hey, you're dif-f'rent too! But we could sit and talk a lit-tle bit

do? I know we're dif - f'rent, but may-be we'd learn

D **B⁷** **D/A** **Em/A** **D**

Last time to Coda ⊕

me and you; _ I could learn a lit-tle bit a-bout you. Would you

some - thing new _ me and you.

verse 1:

G **D** **G** **D**

Person A Person B

1. We speak _ dif-f'rent lan-gaug-es. _ It's hard to pro-nounce your name. _

G **D** **E⁷** **A⁷**

Person A Person B

What do we have to talk _ a-bout? Do we do an-y-thing the same? _ Would you

[NOTE: The verses of this song were not included on the companion recording.]

(continued on next page)

13

Me And You

verse 2: **1.**

G — Older adult — D — Child — G — D

2. I don't know how to talk to child-ren. I'm a ver-y dif-f'rent age than you!___

G — Older adult — D — Child — E⁷ — A⁷

Kids to-day are such a mys-ter-y!___ I don't e-ven know what grown-ups do!___ Would you

verse 3: **2.**

G — Person C — D — Person D — G — D

3. I like___ play-ing base-ball. Hey! Base-ball's my fav-'rite game!___

G — Person C — D — Person D — E⁷ — A⁷

May-be we could hang out___ for a while. It's kind of cool that we're not the same!___ Would you

Coda

D — D/A — Em/A — D — B⁷ — D/A — Em/A — D

you. We could sit and talk a lit-tle bit me and you;___ I could learn a lit-tle bit a-bout you.

you. May-be we'd learn some-thing new___ me and you.

chorus:

1. Would you like a glass of water? Would you like to sit down?
   Would you like to talk a little with me?
   I know I'm different — hey, you're different too!
   But we could sit and talk a little bit, me and you;
   I could learn a little bit about you.

2. Tell me — what's your name?
   What do you like to do?
   I know we're different,
   But maybe we'd learn something new —
   Me and you.

verses:

1. Person A: We speak different languages
   Person B: It's hard to pronounce your name
   Person A: What do we have to talk about?
   Person B: Do we do anything the same?

2. Older adult: I don't know how to talk to children!
   Child: I'm a very different age than you!
   Older adult: Kids today are such a mystery!
   Child: I don't even know what grown ups do!

3. Person C: I like playing baseball.
   Person D: Hey! Baseball's my favorite game!
   Person C: Maybe we could hang out for a while!
   Person D: It's kind of cool that we're not the same!

14

Left, Right

3-part marching round

Words & Music by
Joanne Hammil

♩ = 120

1 Left, left, I al-ways vot-ed left, but now the left seems right — right?

2 They don't even care about chil - dren, or im - mi-grants or health in -sur - ance! What is

Last time to Coda ⊕

3 left? Who is right? I feel left out! Let's turn it a-bout and make a new

⊕ *Coda* **All parts rejoin for Coda**

rit.

Let's turn it a - bout and make a new left!

* This round should be performed while marching in place (left, right), beginning with left foot. Whenever the word "left" is sung, you'll be landing on left foot; when "right" is sung, you'll be landing on right foot. This helps keep you on track as well as add fun.

Left, left, I always voted left, but now the left seems right — right?

— They don't even care about children, or immigrants or health insurance! What is

Left? Who is right? I feel left out! Let's turn it about and make a new left!

HAND MOTIONS – *Add hand motions for more fun and better expression:*
   1st 3 "left"s – raise left fist and punch air
   4th "left" – left palm up and turn head to look at palm
   1st "right" – right palm up and turn head to look at palm
   2nd "right" – both palms up and shrug and look forward questioning (at audience)
   5th "left" – left palm up and turn head to look at palm
   3rd "right" – right palm up and turn head to look at palm
   6th "left" – stick left thumb up and point it backward over left shoulder
   "out" – stick right thumb up and point it backward over right shoulder
   "turn it about" – roll fists around each other in front of body

15

Kate's Full Moon Sing

(written after the first time I participated in one of Kate Munger's rounds sings)

Words & Music by
Joanne Hammil

3-part round

1 Kate brings the wood and the tea, and of course the mu-sic___ for the wo-men. We

2 gath-er on the beach at To-mal-es Bay and the sky is full of our sing-ing.

3 Oo___ full moon, ris-ing like our voic-es to-ge-ther as___ one. When

Kate brings the wood and the tea, and of course the music for the women. We
Gather on the beach at Tomales Bay and the sky is full of our singing!
Oo - oo, full moon, rising like our voices together as one! (When...)

For Pete's Sake

(written in tribute to a true mentor of mine)

Words & Music by
Joanne Hammil

3-part catch

1 Sing out _____ for Pete's sake sing out ___ loud and strong! You can

2 change the words __ and see how we can all make __ new songs! Ev - 'ry

3 wo - man and man, __ ev -'ry gir - l, ev -'ry boy keep on keep - in' on! and

Sing out for Pete's sake, sing out loud and strong! You can

Change the words and see how we can all make new songs! Ev'ry

Woman and man, ev'ry gir-l, ev'ry boy keep on keepin' on! (and...)

17

Don't Give Up

Words & Music by
Joanne Hammil

3-part African-style cyclical song

1. Don't give up — have faith in the people!

2. In the people I see hope for freedom!

3. Believe in the people. We are powerful!

Roll It Over

8-part round

Words by Julé Brennan & Joanne Hammil
Music by Joanne Hammil

♩ = 120

Roll it o - ver, let it go, step on back and you'll see ___ What's the wor - ry? Don't you know — All of life is PLAN B. ___ (So)

Ending: all voices sing

All of life is plan B. ___

Roll it over,

Let it go,

Step on back and you'll

See —

What's the worry?

Don't you know

All of life is PLAN

B. (So...)

©2000 JHO Music · All rights reserved · International Copyright Secured

19

Toshi's Clam Chowder

3-part African-style cyclical song

Words & Music by
Joanne Hammil

1. Toshi's clam chowder is the best I've ever had!

2. Potatoes and onions, spices and clams — oh Toshi's clam chowder....yum!

3. Matzo ball soup is good, but my favorite by far is Toshi's clam chowder!

Morning Rhythms

Words & Music by
Joanne Hammil

3-part rhythm round

Gotta get up, brush my teeth, put on my clothes, eat my breakfast, chew my vitamins.

Pack my bag and get my jacket on, — wait! I almost forgot my lunch! Close call. Hey

Look! There's the bus! Gotta run real fast — bye Mom! Run real fast — bye Dad! I made it! Whew!

Sometimes I Stumble

(written for Ben Tousley, September 1997)

Words & Music by
Joanne Hammil

3-part round

Sometimes I stumble, sometimes I fall, sometimes life throws a curve ball; But

When my spirit isn't enough others have filled me with their love, and

I can carry on — loving strong!

Here I Am!

Words & Music by
Joanne Hammil

4-part round

[NOTE: Chord changes after the first staff are only included as an option for richer accompaniment.]

When do we get to get together?
We always say "Let's make a plan." But
Friends are perhaps the happiest part of my
Life so — here I am!

I Can't Sing

3-part partner song or round

*(Parts I & II were created to polyrhythms
learned in a drumming workshop with Ubaka Hill)*

Words & Music by
Joanne Hammil

1. I can't sing, and you can't sing, and we can't sing so why begin? (2X)

2. I'll play a rhythm, I'll play a rhythm, I'll play a rhythm — that's all I can do! (I'll) (2X)

3. We are singing — not even flat! Three-part singing — imagine that! (2X)

Happy Birthday Round

Words & Music by
Joanne Hammil

4-part round

Happy, happy birthday to Mandy today! Of course you

Don't have to be happy, it's your birthday — you get to say how you

Feel, and what you want — you can be happy or not; but we're your

Friends, and so we're happy for you so we say again "Happy Birthday!"

25

Yes, No

Words & Music by
Joanne Hammil

3-part partner song

♩ = 150

I - Adults, emphatically

| D | | F#m | | Em | A | D |

Yes, yes, yes yes yes!

II - Children 12 and under, just as emphatically

No, no, no, no no no no!

III - Teenagers, with 'attitude'

La - ter, la - ter, leave me a - lone!

1. Yes, yes, yes yes yes!

2. No, no, no, no no no no!

3. Later, later, leave me alone!

26

A Mother's Happiness

3-part round

Words & Music by
Joanne Hammil

A mother, a mother

Is only as happy, only as hap-

-py as her saddest child.

27

Assumptions

Words & Music by
Joanne Hammil

4-part round

1 I think that you think I'm stall-ing a-gain,_____ that

2 may-be to-night we'll be more than just friends. _____

3 You think that I think to-night is the night_____ But we're

4 real-ly both think-ing of say-ing "Good-night!"

All sing at end of round:

Good – night!

I think that you think I'm stalling again, that

Maybe tonight we'll be more than just friends.

You think that I think tonight is the night — but we're

Really both thinking of saying "Goodnight!"

Fuzzy Wuzzy

Words: anonymous
Music by Joanne Hammil

2-part round

♩ = 92 *(gradually increase tempo)*

1 Fuz - zy Wuz - zy was a bear; Fuz - zy Wuz - zy had no hair.

2 Fuz - zy Wuz - zy___ was - n't fuz - zy, was he? No! *Last time to Coda* ⊕

⊕ *Coda* **Both parts sing together:**

Fuz - zy Wuz - zy was - n't fuz - zy, was he? Was he fuz - zy? Was he? No!

was he? Fuz - zy Wuz - zy was - n't fuz - zy, was he? No!

Fuzzy Wuzzy was a bear; Fuzzy Wuzzy had no hair.

Fuzzy Wuzzy wasn't fuzzy, was he? No!

coda:

1. Fuzzy Wuzzy wasn't fuzzy, was he? Was he fuzzy? Was he?

2. Fuzzy Wuzzy wasn't fuzzy, was he?

No!

Easy As Mi Sol Do

Words & Music by
Joanne Hammil

4-part partner song

♩ = 130

1. Do la re sol, sol la ti...
2. Mi mi fa mi fa re...
3. Singin' — it's as easy as mi sol do; doesn't matter what words you know; sing along you'll see; sol la ti sol
4. Sing any words you know; come along and sing any do ti la sol fa mi re sol

ending: Do mi sol do!

30

Hope

2-part round

Words by Emily Dickinson*
Music by Joanne Hammil

1 Hope, hope, hope is the thing with feath-ers___ that perch-es in the soul; and___

2 ___ sings, sings,___ sings the tune without the words,___ and___ nev-er stops at all.

Last time to Coda ⊕

⊕*Coda* **Both parts sing together:**

and___ nev-er stops at all, and___

Repeat and fade

all; and___ nev-er stops at all, and___ nev-er stops at

Hope, hope, hope is the thing with feathers that perches in the soul; And—

— sings, sings, sings the tune without the words, and never stops at all.

*"Hope is the thing with feathers
That perches in the soul
And sings the tune without the words
And never stops at all." – Emily Dickinson

Too Much

Words by Mae West*
Music by Joanne Hammil

4-part round

♩ = 152

Too much, too much, too much, too much of a good thing,

A good thing, too much, too much of a good thing,

Too much of a good thing, too much

Of a good thing — is wonderful!

"Too much of a good thing is wonderful!" – Mae West

32

On The Move

4-part round with changing verses

Words & Music by
Joanne Hammil

♩ = 134

1 B♭   A♭

1. Like my sis - ters be - fore ___ me and my sis - ters to come, I'm on the

2

Like my sis - ters be - fore ___ me and my sis - ters to come ___ I'm on the

3

I know where I come ___ from, ___ know where I'm bound, ___

4   *Last time to Coda* ⊕

Like my sis - ters be - fore ___ me and my sis - ters to come, ___ I'm on the

(1 cont'd)   E♭   B♭

move. ___

(2 cont'd)

move. ___

(3 cont'd)

I'm not a - fraid to break new ground ___ 'cause

(4 cont'd)   **(1)**

move. ___ Like my

(continued on next page)

33

On The Move

sis - ters to come._____ I'm on the move.

1. Like my sisters before me and my sisters to come, I'm on the move.
   Like my sisters before me and my sister to come, I'm on the move.
   I know where I come from, know where I'm bound, I'm not afraid to break new ground
   'Cause like my sisters before me and my sisters to come, I'm on the move.

2. Like my brothers before me and my brothers to come, I won't be still...

3. Like the singers before me and the singers to come, I'm singing loud...

4. Like my Mama before me and my daughter to come, I'll carry on...

5. Like my sisters before me and my sisters to come, I'm on the move...